I0135192

Tales of Elephants

Compiled by Luo Aidong

1 Plus Books
China Pictorial Press

Tales of Elephants

©2017 China Pictorial Press
©2017 1 Plus Books   English Edition

ISBN-13: 978-0-9994263-9-5

English Translator: Zhong Yuanshan
Special Editor: Sophia Liu
Book Design: Ai Qing
Published by 1 Plus Publishing & Consulting in the USA
www.1plusbooks.com
San Francisco, USA

Preface

China faces a heavy task in promoting economic growth as a developing country. Nevertheless, with regard to global climate change and environmental protection, the Chinese government, in recent years, has been advancing a development concept of "innovation, coordination, green, open and sharing", taking green development and a low-carbon and circular economy to the next level. Unprecedented priority has been given to eco-environmental protection. Wild animals are the spirits of nature, and those endangered rare species are very sensitive factors in the eco-environment. With special habits and unique survival wisdom, they harmonize perfectly with the successive beauty of the different seasons and, along with China's diverse geographical environment and rich fauna and flora, constitute the natural environment without which we cannot exist.

China has a long history of thousands of years. It not only

has a profound cultural heritage, but also rich ecological diversity, and a wide variety of wild animals is one of the highlights. China has always been committed to the ecological/environmental cause and has made great progress in the wild animal protection. According to the 2011 National Wildlife Resource Survey, China's rare and endangered wildlife protection has achieved remarkable results: the survival status of a number of endangered wild animals such as the Golden Monkeys, Asian elephants, Père David's deer, giant pandas, crested ibis, Tibetan antelopes, etc., has improved and significant population increases. Among the 420 species listed in the *Lists of Widelife under Special State Protection*, the populations of 341, are no longer considered endangered. At the same time, however, the situation of wildlife protection in China is still very serious, 87.7% of the wild animals are face a squeeze on their living space due to habitat reduction, fragmentation, deterioration, human activity, etc.; many important habitats and bird cluster activity areas and migration channels are challenged by land development, agricultural reclamation, environmental pollution and other threats.

It is of great significance to protect wild animals, save rare and endangered wild animals and maintain biodiversity and ecological balance according to law, for promoting the harmonious development of humans and nature and enhancing the construction of a true ecological civilization. I hope that this colorful, dynamic life pictorial on Chinese wild animals will enable the general adult readers to embark on a unique trip through the natural beauty on Earth, while drawing their attention to the fate of China's rare wild animals and encouraging them to become actively involved in the protection movement along with us. We can build a new pattern of broad participation in wildlife protection and make due contributions to the construction of a beautiful China with a good ecological civilization and improvement of the global environment!

The Compiler

Nov.2017

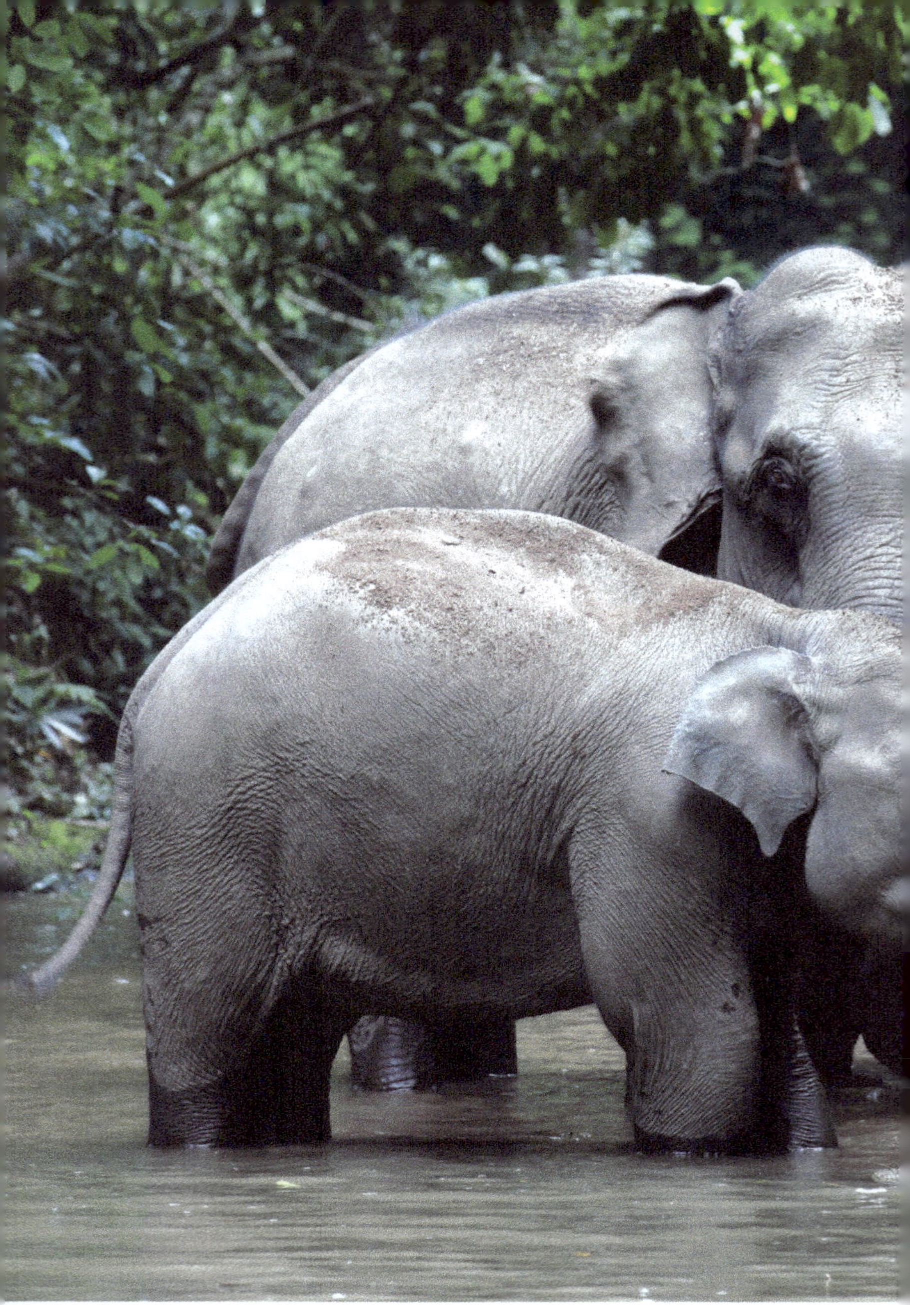

CONTENTS

I

Asian Elephant of China

Asian elephants are the largest living terrestrial animals in the region and the second largest in the world (behind their close relative-the African elephant). They live in tropical and subtropical regions of Asia, mostly valleys, riversides, bamboo forests and broad-leaved mixed forests at elevations of less than 1,000 meters and with dense vegetation and abundant food and water. This book focuses on the wild Asian elephant of China (except for special instructions in this book, the "Asian elephant" is referred to simply as "elephant").

An Asian elephant.

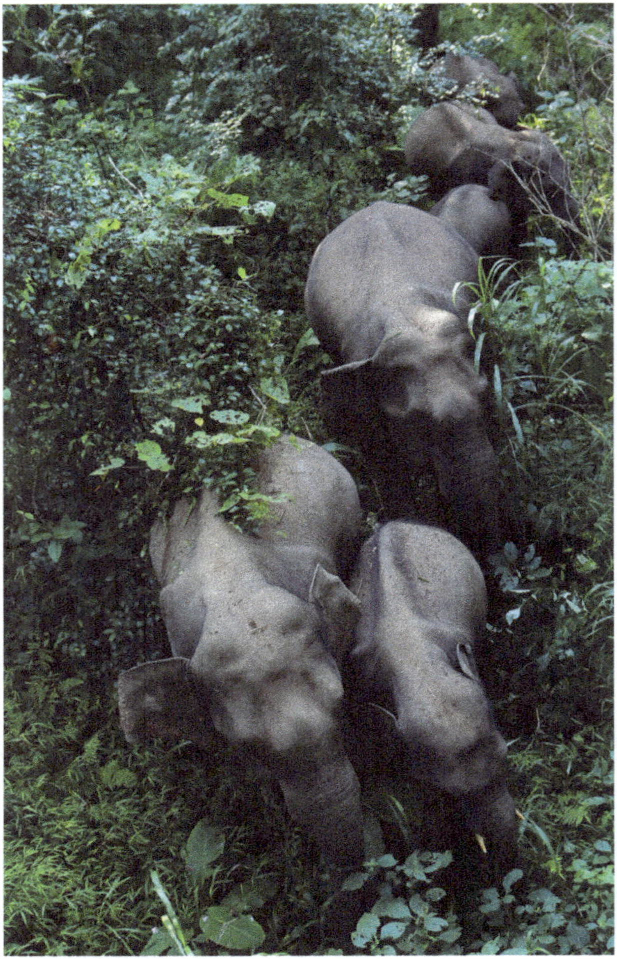

Classification and Status

The Asian elephant (*Elephas maximus*) belongs to the genus Elephas of Elephantoidea in Proboscidea of Mammali in Chordata and is usually also known as a great elephant, old elephant, wild elephant and Indian elephant. Four subspecies are recognized, namely: India elephant (*Elephas maximus indicus*) ,Ceylon elephant (*Elephas maximus maximus*) , Sumatran elephant(*Elephas maximus sumatrensis)* and Borneo pygmy elephant(*Elephas maximus borneensis*).

Distribution

In history, Asian elephants were distributed over a much wider area than today. This included most Asian countries. In China, they appeared more than 3,000 years ago. Today, besides China, people can see elephants in Bangladesh, Bhutan, Brunei, Cambodia, India, Laos, Malaysia,

Myanmar, Nepal, Sri Lanka, Thailand and Vietnam, with the total numbering between 30,000 and 50,000. At present, the wild elephants in China are only found in Xishuangbanna National Nature Reserve, Nangunhe Nature Reserve and Pu'er in Yunnan, with a population of less than 300, below one-seventh of the giant panda populations. It is urgent to adopt protective measures to avoid extinction.

In recent years, China has been working with the international community on intensified efforts to protect elephants. The International Union for the Conservation of Nature (IUCN) has classified Asian elephants as endangered species and the Convention on International Trade in Endangered Species of Wild Fauna and Flora (CITES) has classified them in Appendix I as a species that cannot be traded. The Chinese government classifies them in its first-ranking protected category of wild animals.

• Forests—the last home of elephants.

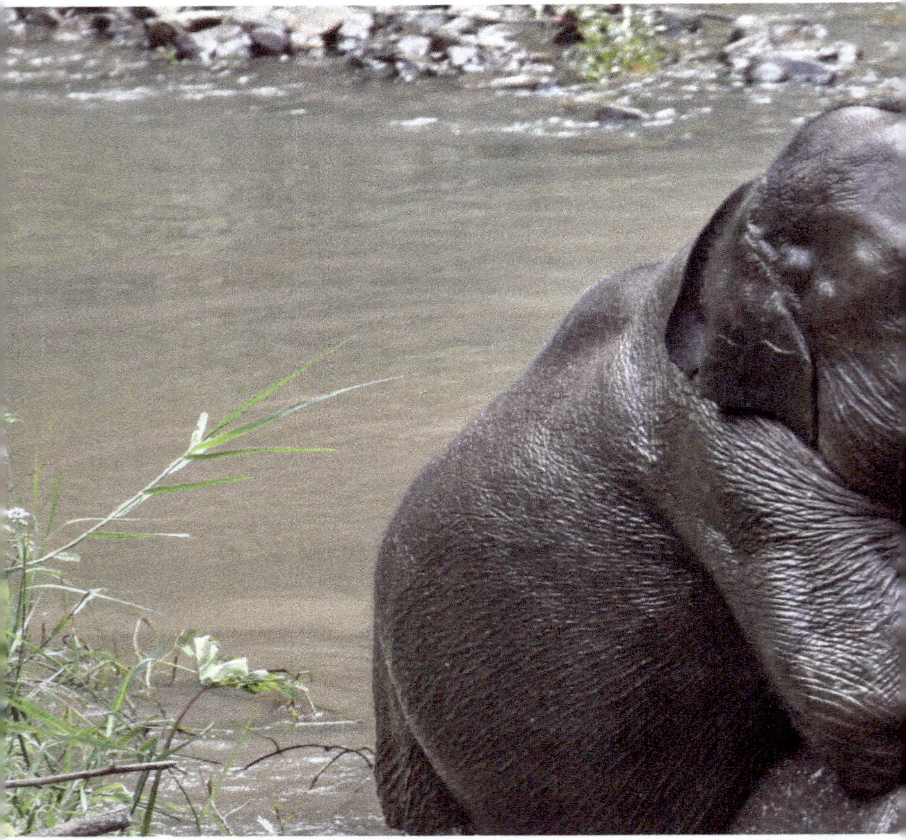

II

Characteristics of
Elephants

Skin

The skin of the elephants is very thick to protect them from being scratched by branches. There is little hair, except for sparsely-distributed rough long hair on the skin helpful for heat dissipation. The skin has many folds some as deep as several centimeters, helping preserve moisture.

• The elephant's skin is distinguished from other animals by its roughness, thickness, and lack of hair.

• Although the skin is thick, sometimes elephants need to apply mud to the body to resist the invasion of forest insects.

Trunk

An elephant's trunk is its most distinctive feature. This may be up to two meters long, so that a drooping trunk can touch the ground. There is a finger-like protrusion on top of the trunk. The trunk contains more than 100,000 sets of muscle allowing the animal to freely twist and perform all kinds of action in a very smart way. In addition to breathing, the trunk also allows the elephant to suck water. The water first stays in the nasal cavity, then pours into the mouth, and is finally swallowed. In hot weather, the elephants can suck and spray water over their body. They can also curl their agile trunks to hold food, and then deliver it to their mouth. The baby elephant can stand up first with the mother's help via her trunk. The finger-like protrusion on the trunk is capable of picking up a small needle on the ground. In circuses or zoos, some specially trained elephants can use their trunks to perform upside down, shake flag sand play the harmonica and other programs. In Thailand, elephants can even use the trunk to paint on a canvas. In addition, the trunk is a common weapon for elephants to fight. With the trunk, the elephant can detect and identify smells from a few thousand meters away.Thanks to the keen sense of smell, they can quickly detect danger and prepare in advance to protect themselves and their family.

• Like a man's hand, the long trunk of the elephants can easily pull down branches from high above the ground.

Ears

An elephant's ear seems like a fan. In fields, elephants often use their ears as a fan to drive away mosquitoes and, more importantly, to help the body discharge heat. There is no sweat gland or pore in the elephant's skin, and so they discharge sweat and body heat mainly by flapping their ears. An ear of an Asian elephant is one-third the size of its head, and the shape seems like the map of Indian mainland, which is why it is also known as the Indian elephant.

• Elephant ears usually look gray and dusty, but in sunshine they become "red ears".

• Typical Asian elephant ears.

▢ Eyes

The eyes of elephants are small, and their
vision weak. There is a saying that, as the
elephant lives in the dense jungle, the line of sight
is covered by trees, and in the long evolutionary
process, vision gradually degenerated. However,
the elephant developed a keen sense of smell
and hearing to make up for lack of vision.
Interestingly, although the elephant's vision
is not very good, it possesses self-cognitive
ability that is rarely seen in other wildlife–it can
"recognize" itself in a mirror. Once researchers
painted a large white mark on the head of three
elephants, and then put them in front of a very
large mirror. The three elephants could actually
"recognize"themselves, and one elephant named
Lele even touched that mark in the mirror with
his trunk repeatedly.

• Elephant eyes sometimes show affectionate, sometimes alertness, and sometimes a naughty cuteness

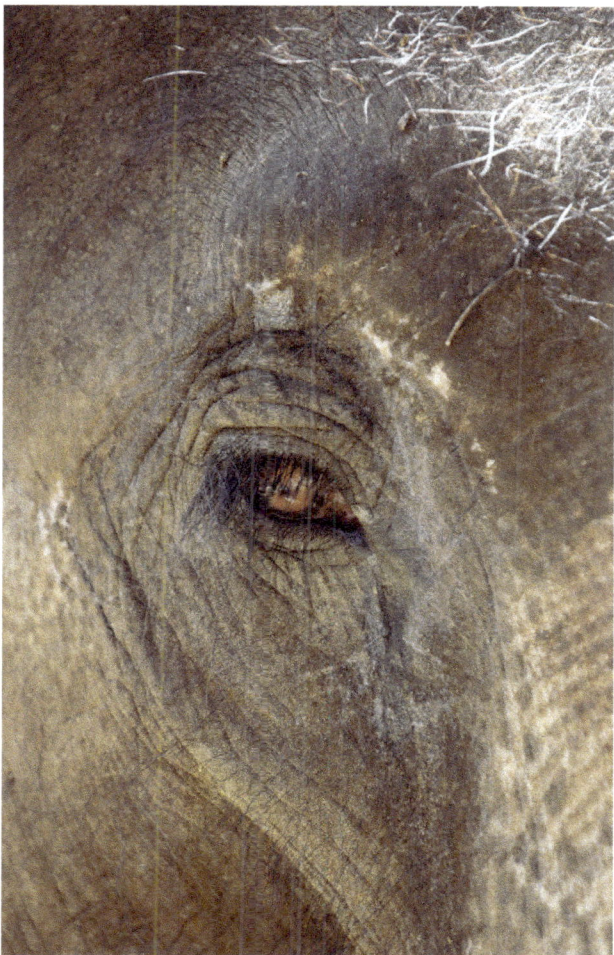

Tusks

The upper incisors of a male Asian elephant protrude outside the lips and tilt upwards, and the hollow tusks are what we usually call "ivory".The upper incisors of a female elephant are smaller and shorter, and generally not exposed outside the mouth. Ivory is mostly milky white or white, and rarely brown due to deposition of some foreign objects. Tusks are a symbol of strength for male elephants. They are important weapon for attack, defense and competition for spouses, and also help to fetch food. The length of an Asian elephant tusk usually ranges from around 10 cm to two meters, and a pair of tusks stored at present in the Siamese National Museum in Bangkokisthe largest amongmodern Asian elephant tusks: the left and the right ones being three meters and 2.74 meters long respectively. Asian elephant tusks are always white, but cannot withstand fine polishing. They are one of the main raw materials of dental carvings. Regardless of the value of the carvings in art collection, the long tusks often bring disaster to elephants, and it is now generally considered wrong to buy or wear ivory products.

• Compared with the male elephants living in Thailand and India, the tusks of those in China are relatively short.

• Some female elephants also have distinctive tusks. This is a femaleliving in the Xishuangbanna Nature Reserve.

• Not all adult male elephants have long tusks as people think. Many, in fact have short tusks.

Tail

Compared with the huge body, the elephant's tail is very short, with only a small amount of hair at the end, like a tail brush. Interestingly, in the field activities, the tail always keeps swinging to drive away mosquitoes; however, because it is so short, it cannot play a big role. Experts speculate that the short tail is the result of living in dense jungle, as, if the tail is too long it could easily snag on branches or bushes, causing inconveniencein activities and even harm.

• Sometimes the tail can also be used as a toy between elephants.

Therefore, in the long process of evolution, the elephant's tail has slowly degenerated, while the hair on the tail has become increasingly scarce.

Limbs

Asian elephant limbs are tall, stout and strong. The forefoot has five toes, and the hind foot has four. It has 19 pairs of ribs and 33 caudal vertebrae.

• The elephant's stout limbs are the fundamental base of its large body.

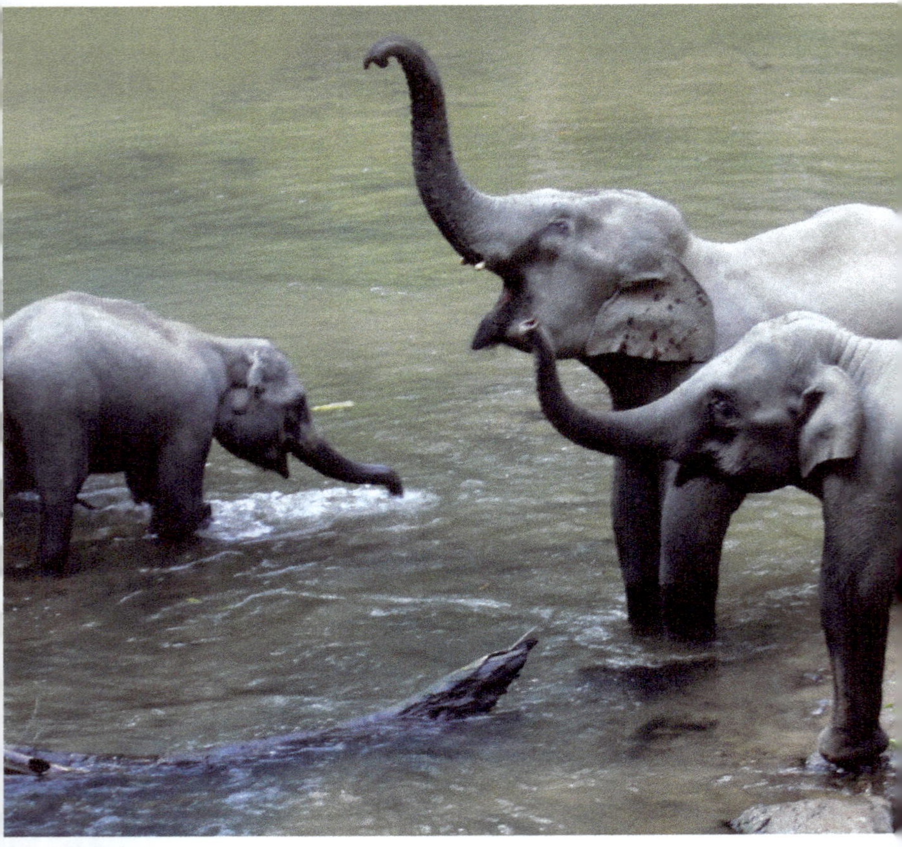

III

Family of Elephants

lephants live in groups, and in the wild natural environment most groups of elephants form families. A group is as small as a couple of elephants and as big as several dozen, and composed of one or more families. The head of an elephant group is a female elephant and the group members include her sisters and children. In the Xishuangbanna National Nature Reserve, a small group consists of only two to three elephants and a big one consists of as many as 20. There are special cases of big groups containing more than 30 elephants through mergers. According to records, a combined group of more than 70 elephants was found near Nanping

Village in the Shang Yongzi Nature Reserve on August 25, 2003. In addition, Asian elephants living in China have relatively rich food sources, and there is no large-scale migration. The most common population in the nature reserve is 6 to 10. Adult male elephants often live alone, so do a few old elephants that have fallen behind.

Up to now, an Indian female elephant named Lakimi Kuti is recognized as the world's longest-living elephant and was crowned as "queen"in 1983. She was born in 1913, and died in 1997, with a lifespan of 84 years.

Female elephants achieving sexual maturity will remain in their original groups, butmale elephants will generally be driven out of the group to live separately, and as a result they have the opportunity to mate in other groups. From the genetic point of view, this can avoid inbreeding, reduce disease, and ensure that genes of different groups can be fully communicated, which is conducive to population growth.

Elephants do not have a fixed residence. They have a wide range of activities, but will spend up to 16 hours a day looking for food. Often, an adult has an average activity range of at least 10 square kilometers.

Researchers have found that elephant populations break up and reunite at times. In general, different groups are relatively independent in their activities, with little overlap. However, there are some big gatherings composed of several small groups. Such a big group is not stable and a combined group will soon break up into smaller, more stable groups. Usually a combined group with close kinship will remain stable for a relatively longer time.

• There is no adult male elephant in a typical Asian elephant family.

• Through a year, an adult male elephant will live with different families at odd times to seek the chance of mating.

• In 2011, a combined group of 30 elephants was found at the edge of the Shangxiongzi Nature Reserve in the Xishuangbanna Nature Reserve.

• In the Wild Elephant Valley in the Xishuangbanna Nature Reserve, people can often see combined groups of 20 to 30 elephants.

IV

Behavior and Wisdom
of Elephants

◻ Foraging

Elephants are herbivorous animals with no fixed feeding time. They can be seen foraging in the morning, at noon or in the evening. Elephant digestibility is not high, and only about 40% of the food can be absorbed, so they spend most of the day looking for nutrition. In the forest, the elephants usually eat while relieving their bowels, so that a lot of undigested plant seeds are spread to different places with the elephant's movement. Therefore, the elephant plays an important role in the forest ecosystem–spreading the seeds and promoting forest renewal.

- Foraging is the main daily activity. They have no other choice cue to their huge body and low digestion rate

- Elephants feed on bamboo leaves.

Activity Routines

Elephants are afraid of heat, and they are sensitive to changes in the temperature of their habitat. In summer, it is very hot during daytime and they like to rest in shady valley woods to avoid exposure. They usually forage in the early morning or at nightfall when it is relatively cool.

• An elephant group in a shady wood.

• The Lancangjiang River system with rich water resources
is the source of happiness for Asian elephants living in
Xishuangbanna.

Drinking Water

An elephant has to drink 150 to 200 kilograms
of water a day. Drinking water is the most
important activity next only to foraging. The
elephants living in Xishuangbanna drink water
at odd time and in unfixed places as long as
condition permit.

☐ Bathing

   Elephants like to live by waters. In addition to drinking water, they often go to the river and take a bath to cool down in the hot summer. Bathing is an important part of elephant life. In hot sunshine, in order to reduce the body temperature, an elephant will use its long trunk to suck water, and then spray it over the entire body. They will also dive into the water like humans and try to immerse the whole body in the water. However, if the river is not deep enough, which is common, they can only immerse the head and trunk, and the back and most of the body is high above the water surface like a hill. Then, smart elephants will roll in the water, so that every part of the body is also immersed in the cool water and they can enjoy coolness in summer!

- In addition to water, a mud bath is also a way for cooling and avoiding mosquito-bites.

- Elephants bathing in the water.

Moving

The elephant's athletic ability is very strong. In addition to long marches of hundreds and even thousands of kilometers, they can run quickly. Due to its large size, the elephant cannot run for long time or long distance, and its stamina is poorer than other large mammals. The two feet on a same side of an elephant step forward at the same time, known as "slippery", which is different from other mammals and looks somewhat funny. Because of this, the elephant on the move can maintain minimum movement of the center of gravity. It is also a reason elephants with such a large size can consume less energy than other animals.

• Regardless of the large size and heavy body, an elephant can run at a speed of 40 kp/h. Therefore, it is best to observe a wild elephant at a safe distance of at least 100 meters.

• Fighting is often seen between male elephants.

Fight and Play

Elephants like to play and fight. In an elephant group, for the sake of showing a dominant position, courtship and other reasons, the male elephants often chase and fight each other. Under normal circumstances, the height, weight and trunk length area prerequisite for victory.

• Elephants also have a naughty nature.

• Touching another's long trunk is the most common way for Asian elephants to communicate and promote emotions.

Communication

Scientists found that elephants can identify more than 100 kinds of calls from their league. The elephants communicate with each other mainly by infrasonic wave that humans cannot hear. The roar of elephants heard by human beings is usually only a small part of the way of communication. The elephant has a high IQ and rich emotion. As a social animal, members with different status and division of labor in a group work together under a "leader".They are attached to each other, convey a variety of information through sound (mostly infrasonic waves), smell and physical contact, and maintain the intimacy and cohesion among families.

Alertness

In every group, there is an elephant whose full-time responsibility is for alert. This is known as the "guard elephant". In group activities, a guard elephant is in charge of guarding, raising the alarm, and even attacking. Usually a guard elephant is not involved in group activities. It keeps a distance from the group. When some threats appear imminent, it will use sounds to immediately alert the group who will immediately maintain high vigilance. Except for the breeding season, most of the roars made by wild elephants in the jungle are the alerts from guard elephants having discovered an abnormal situation. In addition, Asian elephants often beat the ground with their trunk and issue a low roarin the foraging place, which means a declaration of territorial ownership and warning to other elephants: "I am the master here. Keep away!"

• In group activities, a guard elephant is always on the alert.

☐ Wisdom

The elephants in captivity in Sri Lanka and India can make a variety of modeling and cute gestures under the guidance of elephant trainers. Thai elephants can use their trunks like man's hand and hold a brush to paint. In some South Asian countries people often train elephants for service. The following story from the Xishuangbanna Nature Reserve fully embodies the elephants' "thinking"ability and wisdom.

One day, a group of 16 wild elephants came from the hillside to the river bend at the Wild Elephant Valley to play and drink water.A coconut drifted down the river to the group, and a small elephant in the group began to use its trunk to remove the coconut from the river to the sandyshore. It first sniffed it with its trunk, and then gently kicked it back and forth with its feet. People thought that the elephant would play with the coconut just like a ball. Surprisingly, the elephant seemed to smell the sweetness of the coconut milk.It constantly touched the coconut with the tip of its trunk, intending to get the coconut milk inside, only to be stopped by the hard shell.The delicious food at hand was hard to get at. The animal thought for a while. Then, it held the coconut with its trunk, put one foot on it, seeking to to crush the shell. However, because the coconut was placed on the soft sand, the weight of one foot was not enough. Then the animal got up and moved the weight of the body to the coconut. Failure! What to do? Place one more foot. Enough! Let me stand on it with my whole body. With a sharp crack, the coconut broke. The small elephant finally got the sweet coconut milk with its "wisdom".

The puzzle is the small elephant had never seen a coconut, and yet it finally broke the shell with both feet. How could it get the idea? Is it an instinct, or on-site learning? It seems that wildlife in nature is much smarter than we think, and there are a lot of mysteries to be solved!

• How to break it?

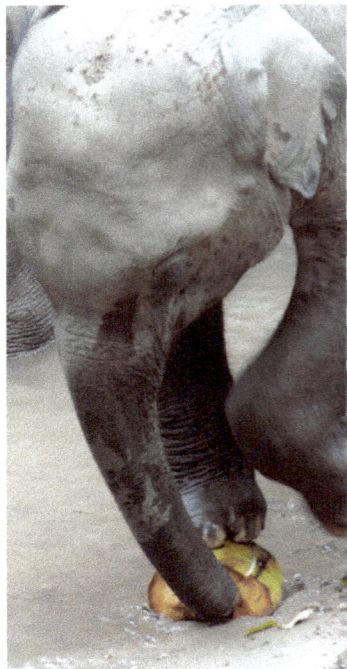

• Does it work by stepping on it?

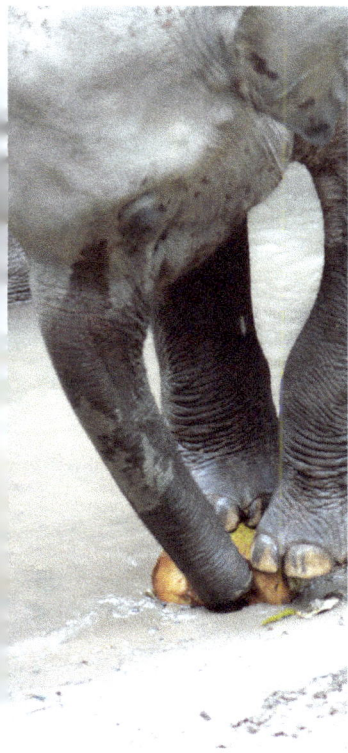

• One foot is enough for such a small one.

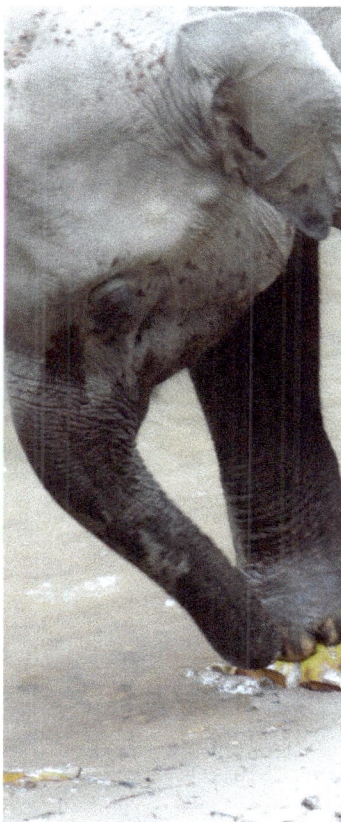

• Use two feet. Okay this time!

☐ Learning and Memory

In order to prevent elephants from invading people's crops, the relevant departments in Xishuangbanna National Nature Reserve began to adopt a preventive measure by setting up solar-energy electric fences in 1990. Over time, some elephants actually learned to lift their both feet, and then step their insulated soles on the live electric fence. They know that this could help them avoid electric shock and get access to farmland. This experience is firmly remembered by the elephants. After 20 years, the solar-energy electric fences were abandoned in the nature reserve, but some elephants still "remembered"the experience and continued to practicetheir skill: as long as there appears something like wire in front, they will step on it with their soles. It confirms a well-known Western proverb: An elephant never forgets.

• A wire in front, so be careful!

• According to experience, I will not be shocked by electricity as long as I lift my feet and step on the wire.

V

Reproduction of Elephants

Estrus

Adolescence for elephants starts at an age between seven and 10; by the age of 14, the elephants in Xishuangbanna generally achieve sexual maturity. In estrus and during the mating season, female elephants will experience a significant change in their bodies:A liquid substance is secreted by the sexual gland, the labia become everted and red and swollen, and the secretion increases. Male elephants will show symptom of urine incontinence; the temporal glands on both sides of the head will secrete a liquid substance, and the penis will be erect and exposed during the active time. Both male and female elephants are very irritable during estrus, and sometimes will even attack members of the family (there are cases showing elephants in captivity will attack their owners at this time). Male elephants will be involved in fighting for a mate, but few will break their tusks or die of serious injury due to the fighting.

• Adult male elephants lock for spouses.

• Two adult male elephants fight over a mate.

Mating

Mating generally occurs once a year, more often in early Spring, and the season lasts for two to three months. Mating can be seen occasionally in other seasons, when the probability of successful pregnancy is not high. Before mating, the two elephants forming a couple caress each other through smelling, touching, intertwining trunks, curling body and snuggling and blowing in a love prelude. After a successful mating, the female elephant undergoes a gestation period of 20 to 22 months. The female gives birth to one baby, only very occasionally twins. The life expectancy for Asian elephants is 60 to 80 years generally. In the wild state, for various reasons, a female gives birth every six to eight years, meaning an average of four births in a lifetime.

Farrowing

In the pre-labor period, in order to facilitate the production of cubs and prepare enough foods for postpartum, the female will find places rich in food and covered with soft soil.

Baby elephants can stand up slowly only one or two hours after birth. A newborn baby has distinctive fetal hair and its trunk is 25 to 35 cm long, with a height of 76 to 91 cm and a weight of about 100 kg. The baby elephant can follow its mother to forage one or two days after birth.

In an elephant herd, if there is a pregnant mother present, her companions will always accompany her, not leaving because of her difficulty in moving. They will forage nearby. After birth and once the baby can walk and follow the mother, the whole herd will leave together. The behavior of feeding and caring for offspring can be seen in Asian elephants. The baby elephants are fed with milk for three years or so, and then weaned.

• Baby elephants in a family will get the most care and protection: the adults always surround the babies in the center.

• A newborn baby reveals its love of water.

• Just a few hours after the birth, a baby elephant can walk around its mother.

☐ Homosexuality

Researchers in the Xishuangbanna Nature Reserve found after years of observation that the male elephants living in Xishuangbanna displayed "homosexual" tendencies, and this phenomenon usually occurs in non-mating seasons. It can be seen between two adults or between an adult and near-adult elephant.

• Intimacy between two adult male elephants.

VI

Food of Elephants

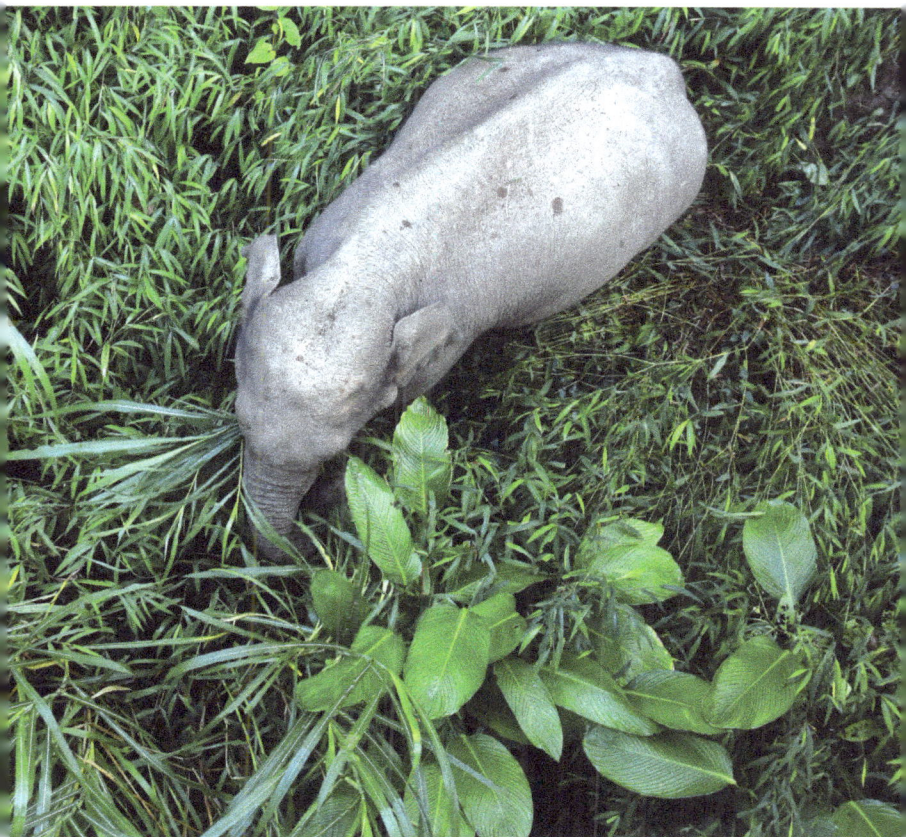

Foraging

With their great size, elephants have a huge
appetite. An adult tends to eat about 150
kilograms of various foods every day. Elephants
in the wild can forage for a wide range of plants,
including plant shoots, leaves, stems and so on.
The recipe of Asian elephants in Xishuangbanna
contains more than 100 kinds of plants covering
a dozen of plant families such as banana,
Gramineae, palmae, Moraceae, Araliaceae and
Vitaceae. Bamboo, wild bananas, tigergrass and
palmae plants are favorites. In addition, the Asian
elephants also like to eat ripe rice plants, bananas,

sugar cane and other crops, and occasionally they leave forest and go to villages for foraging fruits, melons and vegetables.

• Broussonetia papyrifera.

• Tigergrass.

- The bark of many tropical rainforest trees are also foods of Asian elephants.

- Wild bananas are one of the favorite foods of Asian elephants.

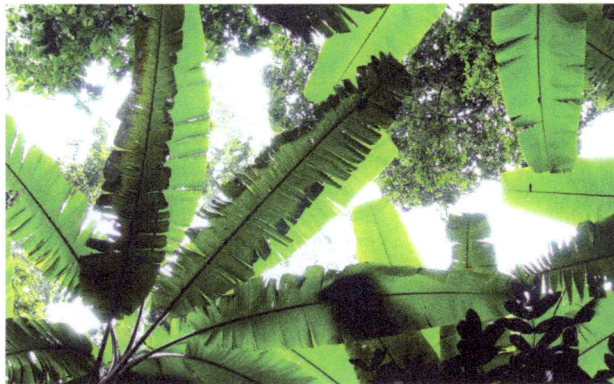

Foraging Routines

Bush, grass, bamboo and forest are the main foraging areas. Asian elephants have a huge appetite, and after the elephants have fed, it takes one or more months for new plants to begin growing. Therefore, the elephants will not stay in one place for a long time.After foraging for a while, they will often move on and then return after several months, allowing the forests and plants enough time for re-growth. The elephants migrate in accordance with the growth of their food sources, which is a result of a long-term evolution. It benefits the health of the forest ecosystem and ensures that the elephants are well-fed.

• Constantly moving is an effective way for the elephants to get enough foods.

VII

Living Environment
of Elephants

F ood, water and good hidden places are the main considerations for elephants in choosing habitats. People can see herds of elephants in the four seasons of the year along the Wild Elephant Valley in the Xishuangbanna Nature Reserve in Yunnan, thanks to these factors. It is the best place for observing wild Asian elephants in China.

Due to the large appetite, the elephants move over a very wide range. The habitat for a group of three to five elephants usually covers 20 square km at least, and a larger group needs even more space. The range of habitats mainly depends on group size and the seasons. Sometimes, due to environmental changes or lack of food, there will be more than one group in a same habitat (or an overlapping area to a certain extent).

Elephants do not like high altitudes. They generally like to live at places below 1,300 meters, with humid air, close to water, and forests with dense vegetation. Bamboo forests, monsoon rainforests and monsoon evergreen broad-leaved forests with a wide variety of plants are most frequented. Elephants are also seen hovering around the plantation areas in some villages at the edge of the nature reserve.

• Elephants sometimes hover around the villages at the edge of forests.

• Xishuangbanna–forest home of elephants.

• Forests with low altitude, close to water, and with dense vegetation are ideal habitats.

• The edges of forests are also rich in foods for elephants.

VIII

Companions of
Elephants in Forests

Asian elephants are large in size and live in habitats covering wide areas. In the natural environment where they survive, there are few natural enemies. They have many accompanying wild animals in their habitats, and they live together in peace. These animals include national key protected animals, such as white-limb buffalos, Indochinese tigers, red slender loris, lesser mouse-deer, Rhesus monkeys, pangolins, jackals and black bears, and mammals such as civet cats, big and small civets, jungle cats, sambars, Indian muntjac, Capricornis milneedwardsii and Ratufa bicolor, as well as typical tropical birds such as green peacocks, gray peacock pheasants, hornbills, and sun birds.

• A white-limb buffalo(national first-ranking protected species).

- A wild gray peacock pheasant (national first-ranking protected species).

- A long-beak catching-spider bird (typical tropical bird in Xishuangbanna).

- Great Hornbill (national second-ranking protected wild animal, known as the love bird in rainforests).

- A white-cheek gibbon (national first-ranking protected species).

- A lesser mouse-deer (national first-ranking protected species).

- Rhesus monkeys (national second-ranking protected species).

- A red slender loris (national first-ranking protected species).

- A three-toed Kingfisher (rare species living in the Xishuangbanna rainforests)

IX

Beautiful Homes
Shared by Human and
Elephants

The elephant in the wild is an excellent "ecosystem engineer" that can transform the surrounding physical environment to a great extent through its own activities, playing an important role in maintaining ecosystem stability.

Human-Elephant Harmony

The wild Asian elephants living in the Xishuangbanna Nature Reserve sometimes "venture" into the scenic area, bringing surprises to visitors. The elephants in captivity can also bring endless joy to visitors: elephant pyramid, taking the single-plank bridge, standing upside down, playing football and other programs arouse people's interests in the species.

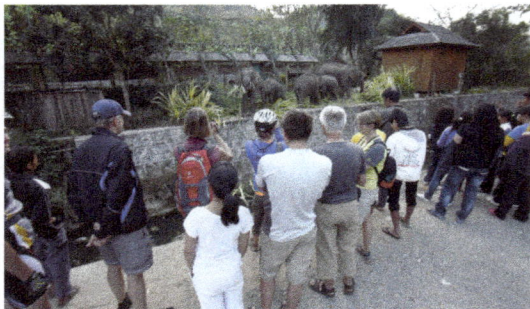

• Wild elephants venture into the scenic area, and lucky tourists can enjoy the view across the river.

Human-Elephant Conflict

With the growth of the human population and the need to develop the economy, agricultural lands continue to expand into the habitats of elephants. As a result, there has been rapid forest reduction with accompanying decline in elephant habitats, and the conflict for living space between human and elephants becomes ever more intensified.

Human destruction of the elephant's habitats and the hunting of elephants occur occasionally.

• The elephant is an important window for people to understand the rainforests in Xishuangbanna.

In Xishuangbanna, from 1994 to 1995 alone, l6 elephants were poached.

Due to the rapid growth of human population, the distance between people and elephants is narrowing, and contradictions and conflicts are increasing. Asian elephants often leave the forests and enter villages, causing harm. They break into the plantation areas to steal and destroy crops, and even damage the farmhouse or other farm facilities, resulting in huge economic losses to local residents.

In order to alleviate the situation, the local government usually offers compensation to residents suffering accidental losses by wild animals. They also tried to build solar-energy electric fences, ditches, and walls to prevent invasion. In particular, in the areas within the nature reserve and the surrounding activity habitats of elephants, management built food source bases for elephants to avoid clashes with humans.

In recent years, the local government has also promulgated forestry policies and laws on protection of wild animals, implemented the natural forest protection project, and taken great efforts to carry out long-term confiscation of civilian firearms. As a result, the poaching of wild animals in the nature reserve has been effectively restrained, and the protection and management on elephants has been strengthened continuously. In 2011, the Xishuangbanna National Nature Reserve authority signed a "Public Liability Insurance on Asian Elephants" with the Pacific Insurance Company, the first its kind in the world. For the first time, local residents can apply for compensation covering property losses from the depredations of elephants and other wild animals in the nature reserve through commercial insurance and government payments.

• Corn field invaded by elephants.

• Farmhouses around forests occasionally become targets of elephant attack.

- Vehicles driving on the highways or parked along roads are also targets of elephant attack.

- In order to gain a better understanding of the routines of the elephants, the workers in the nature reserve often take risks in carrying out observations and making field records.

X

Worries and Appeals:
Protecting the Environment
and Elephants

Crackdown on Poaching

Poaching is the greatest threat to the elephants. On January 6, 2005, a heart-breaking and unforgettable event concerning a mother elephant and her baby occurred in the Xishuangbanna Nature Reserve. The mother elephant was shot at the border area between China and Laos. Disregarding her injuries, she brought the newborn baby to the edge of the nature reserve. Then the mother died and the baby bent over the mother wailing endlessly. The baby elephant did not allow people to approach its mother and tried its best to drive them away, while pushing its mother with its trunk …

• The baby elephant lay beside the mother not knowing she had passed away.

Ban on Ivory Sales

A total ban on ivory sales is a powerful move to protect wild elephants.

▢ Establishing Nature Reserves

Since 1958, the Chinese Government has established a number of nature reserves in the habitats of Asian elephants, such as Xishuangbanna, Lincang, Pu'er and other prefectures and cities, where the species is found. The protection of the wild population and habitats is carried out in all aspects.

Building Food Source Bases: Since 2005, the Xishuangbanna Mengyangzi Nature Reserve has started the construction of 2-square-km food source bases for wild Asian elephants in Lianhuatang, Shulinzhai and Guanping. Plants such as bamboo, wild bananas and palms are grown there, as well as sugar cane and other crops. Every year, from July to September, as the crops mature, wild elephants frequent the food source bases, which is beneficial for the surrounding villagers to harvest crops with interference.

• A herd of elephants enjoyforaging in a food source base in the Xishuangbanna National Nature Reserve.

Rescuing Asian Elephants: In the tropical jungles, young and frail wild elephants often suffer injury. In this case, people seek to rescue injured wild elephants and give them special care, so that they can return to the rainforests after recovery. It is one of the important means of protection on Asian elephants.

At the same time, China has also established the Asian elephant breeding and research center in Xishuangbanna, and actively carries out monitoring of the dynamic changes in wild Asian elephant distribution, population numbers and living environment. They have carried out studies on the behavior, ecology, physiology and genetics of Asian elephants, which provide a scientific basis for the protection and management of the species.

Actively Promoting the Protection and Security of Asian Elephants: To strengthen the

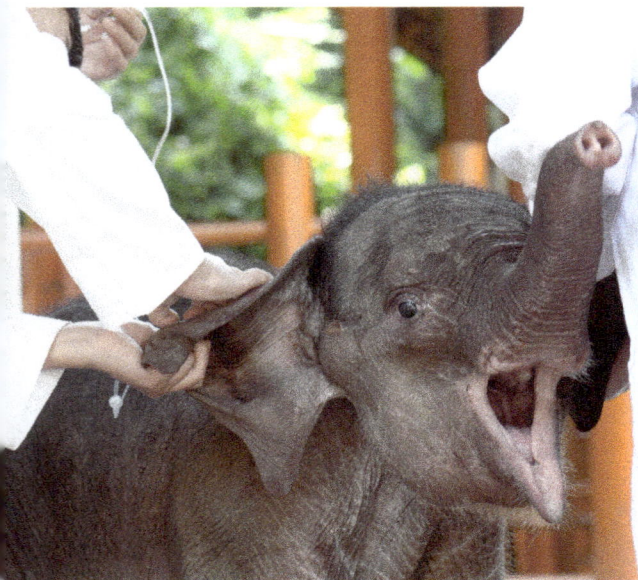

• An injured baby elephant under the care of the staff of the Elephant Breeding Center in the Xishuangbanna National Nature Reserve.

protection of Asian elephants, alleviate human-elephant conflicts, and safeguard human safety and property, the Xishuangbanna National Nature Reserve Administration and the International Fund for Animal Welfare (IFAW) have started long-term cooperation in the active promotion and education on protection of Asian elephants in villages, schools and scenic areas.

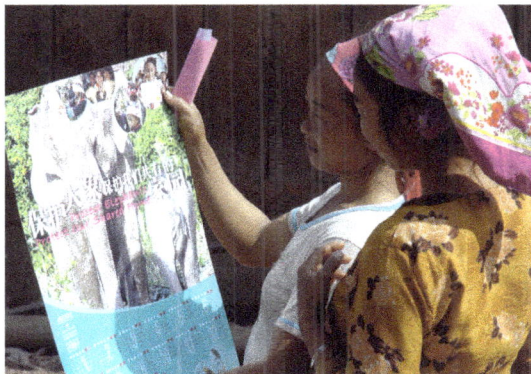

• Residents in surrounding areas of the nature reserve browse the publicity pictures on protection of Asian elephants.

www.ingramcontent.com/pod-product-compliance
Lightning Source LLC
Chambersburg PA
CBHW042249040426
42336CB00043B/3365